WHALES SET I

BLUE WHALES

Megan M. Gunderson
ABDO Publishing Company

Published by ABDO Publishing Company, 8000 West 78th Street, Edina, Minnesota 55439. Copyright © 2011 by Abdo Consulting Group, Inc. International copyrights reserved in all countries. No part of this book may be reproduced in any form without written permission from the publisher. The Checkerboard Library™ is a trademark and logo of ABDO Publishing Company.

Printed in the United States of America, North Mankato, Minnesota.
042010
092010

 PRINTED ON RECYCLED PAPER

Cover Photo: Photolibrary
Interior Photos: © Doc White / SeaPics.com p. 15; National Geographic Stock pp. 5, 11; Peter Arnold pp. 8, 21; © Phillip Colla / SeaPics.com pp. 13, 17; Photo Researchers p. 19; Uko Gorter pp. 7, 9

Editor: Tamara L. Britton
Art Direction & Cover Design: Neil Klinepier

Library of Congress Cataloging-in-Publication Data

Gunderson, Megan M., 1981-
 Blue whales / Megan M. Gunderson.
   p. cm. -- (Whales)
 Includes index.
 ISBN 978-1-61613-447-1
 1. Blue whale--Juvenile literature. I. Title.
 QL737.C424G86 2011
 599.5'248--dc22
                                    2010006441

CONTENTS

BLUE WHALES AND FAMILY

Blue whales are the largest animals that have ever lived on Earth. They are even more massive than the biggest dinosaurs were. A blue whale's tongue alone weighs as much as an elephant!

These gigantic creatures are mammals. Blue whales are **warm-blooded** and nurse their young. They live in the ocean, but surface to breathe air above water.

Blue whales are closely related to several other **cetaceans**. They are members of the family Balaenopteridae. Whales in this family are called rorquals. Humpback whales, minke whales, fin whales, sei whales, and Bryde's whales are all rorquals.

The word rorqual *means* "tubed whale" or "pleated whale." It refers to the long folds on a rorqual whale's throat.

SHAPE, SIZE, AND COLOR

The blue whale has a large head and body. Its tiny dorsal fin is set back toward the flukes. The blue whale breathes through two blowholes located on top of its head. There is a large splashguard in front of the blowholes. It prevents water from entering them.

In the Southern **Hemisphere**, female blue whales average 89 feet (27 m) long. Males reach about 82 feet (25 m) in length. Blue whales weigh up to 400,000 pounds (180,000 kg). Those in the Northern Hemisphere are smaller.

A blue whale's body is **mottled** gray. This spotting ends near the shoulders, so the head

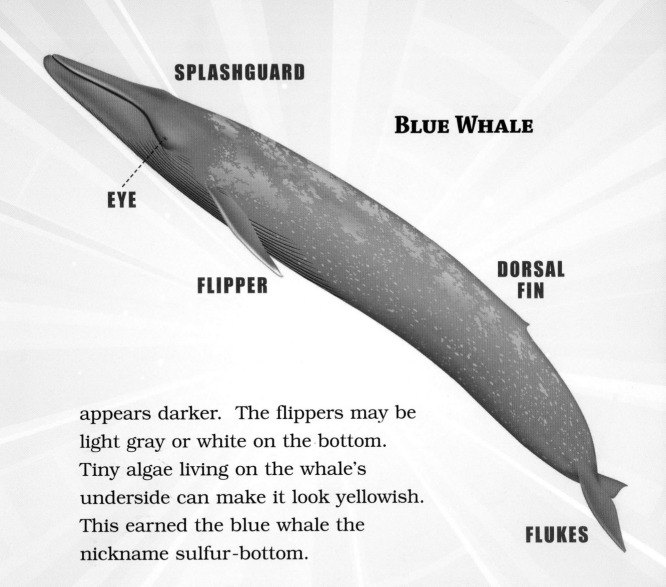

SPLASHGUARD

BLUE WHALE

EYE

FLIPPER

DORSAL FIN

FLUKES

appears darker. The flippers may be light gray or white on the bottom. Tiny algae living on the whale's underside can make it look yellowish. This earned the blue whale the nickname sulfur-bottom.

WHERE THEY LIVE

Blue whales live in all of Earth's oceans. They swim in coastal areas as well as far out to sea. Populations in the Northern **Hemisphere** do not **overlap** with those in the Southern Hemisphere.

Migrating is an important part of life for most blue whales. They move toward the **equator** in winter. There, they breed in warm waters. Blue whales move back

A blue whale's huge flukes move it through its habitat.

8

Where Do Blue Whales Live?

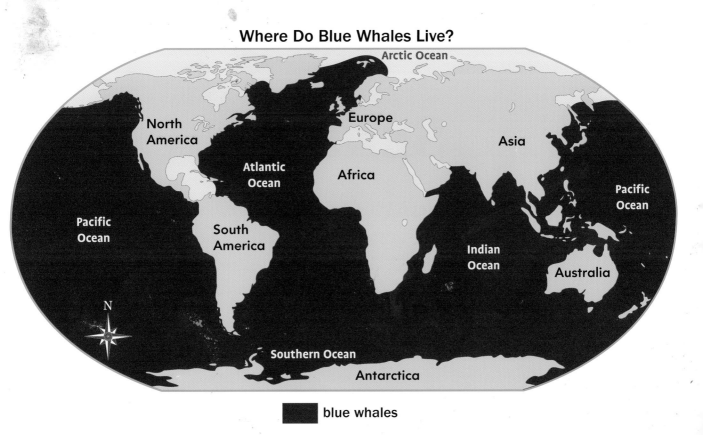

blue whales

toward the **poles** for summer. They do most of their feeding in these cooler waters.

Scientists still have much to learn about blue whale **migration**. For example, blue whales in the northern Indian Ocean seem to follow a different pattern.

SENSES

Scientists believe blue whales rely most on sight and hearing. They are still learning about the senses of taste, smell, and touch in blue whales.

Blue whales have special eye features that help them see in low light. This is important in dark, deep ocean waters.

These huge whales must also communicate in their vast **habitat**. Blue whales aren't just the biggest animals on Earth. They are also the loudest! Their deep, low sounds can be heard hundreds of miles away. So, a good sense of hearing is a vital part of communication.

A blue whale's sounds may also help with navigation. Scientists do not know if blue whales use echolocation. But, they do send out series of

clicks. These bounce off underwater land features.
The returning echoes may tell the blue whale about
its surroundings.

Blue whales may use their loud sounds to identify and greet one another.

DEFENSE

Blue whales do not have many natural predators. Only killer whales and large sharks will attack these huge animals. When in danger, blue whales may try to swim away. They can travel up to 30 miles per hour (48 km/h)!

Long ago, the blue whale's size and speed protected it from humans. In the 1800s, there were about 350,000 blue whales worldwide. Then, whale hunting equipment improved and whaling increased. Now, just 10,000 to 25,000 blue whales remain.

Today, the blue whale is **endangered**. It is protected from most hunting. But, humans are still a threat. Blue whales accidentally become trapped in fishing nets. They are also struck by large ships. And, water pollution harms their **habitat**. Scientists are working hard to protect the blue whale's future.

Some blue whales have scars from killer whale attacks or ship strikes.

FOOD

Amazingly, the biggest animals on Earth don't eat the biggest food. Instead, blue whales feast on tiny creatures called krill. Most krill are less than two inches (5 cm) long! Blue whales eat thousands of pounds of krill a day.

How do blue whales gather so much food? They are **baleen** whales. So, they don't have teeth. Instead, up to 400 baleen plates line each side of the upper jaw. The plates are black and lined with thick, coarse **bristles**.

To feed, a blue whale gulps water and food into its mouth. Then, its tongue pushes the water out through the baleen. The baleen works like a strainer. It retains all the food, which the whale then swallows.

Sometimes, a blue whale swims on its side to feed. Its throat expands to take in huge amounts of water and food.

BABIES

Blue whales reproduce every two to three years. Breeding takes place in winter. Afterward, a female blue whale is **pregnant** for 10 to 12 months. She usually gives birth to one baby each time. Twins are rare.

A baby blue whale is called a calf. It is already huge at birth, measuring 23 to 26 feet (7 to 9 m) long. It weighs 6,000 to 7,900 pounds (2,700 to 3,600 kg).

A mother blue whale nurses her calf for about seven months. During this time, the calf gains 200 pounds (90 kg) every day! Still, the young blue whale takes many years to reach its full size. Scientists think some blue whales have lived as long as 110 years!

Blue whale calves are usually born in winter.

BEHAVIORS

Blue whales fascinate whale watchers. When these huge creatures surface to breathe, they make a loud sound. Breathing out also creates a spout, or blow. This tall, visible cloud of air can reach 30 feet (9 m) high!

Viewers may also see blue whales slap their flippers or flukes on the water's surface. Blue whales **breach**, too. This creates a big splash!

When diving, these massive whales lift their huge flukes out of the water. Most dives take them 500 to 650 feet (150 to 200 m) below the surface. These dives last for 5 to 20 minutes.

Blue whales usually spend time alone or in pairs. When **migrating**, two or three may travel together. Groups of more than 50 gather when feeding.

Young blue whales breach more often than older blue whales.

    Alone or in groups, blue whales are special members of Earth's oceans. Scientists know there is still more to learn about them. These beautiful giants remain mysterious!

BLUE WHALE FACTS

Scientific Name: *Balaenoptera musculus*

Common Name: Blue whale

Other Names: Sibbald's rorqual, sulfur-bottom

Average Size:
Length - 82 to 89 feet (25 to 27 m)
Weight - up to 400,000 pounds (180,000 kg)

Where They Are Found: In all of Earth's oceans

On a clear day, a blue whale will appear turquoise under the water's surface.

GLOSSARY

baleen - the tough, hornlike material that hangs from the upper jaw of certain whales. Whales use baleen to filter food.

breach - to jump or leap up out of water.

bristle (BRIH-suhl) - a short, stiff hair.

cetacean (sih-TAY-shuhn) - a member of the order Cetacea. Mammals such as dolphins, whales, and porpoises are cetaceans.

endangered - in danger of becoming extinct.

equator - an imaginary circle around the middle of Earth. It is halfway between the North and South poles.

habitat - a place where a living thing is naturally found.

hemisphere - one half of Earth.

migrate - to move from one place to another, often to find food.

mottled - marked with spots or blotches of different colors.

overlap - to occupy the same area in part.

pole - either end of Earth's axis. The North Pole and the South Pole are opposite each other.

pregnant - having one or more babies growing within the body.

warm-blooded - having a body temperature that is not much affected by surrounding air or water.

WEB SITES

To learn more about blue whales, visit ABDO Publishing Company on the World Wide Web at **www.abdopublishing.com**. Web sites about blue whales are featured on our Book Links page. These links are routinely monitored and updated to provide the most current information available.

INDEX